TABLE OF CONTENTS

READINESS SKILLS

AND MORE...

DOWNHILL RACE

Practice tracing slanted lines from **left** to **right**.

Practice tracing slanted lines from **right** to **left**.

COOKING CURVES

Practice tracing **curved** lines.

ALL AROUND

Practice tracing **circles**.

SIX SHAPES

Learn the **shapes** by tracing the dotted lines.

Circle

Diamond

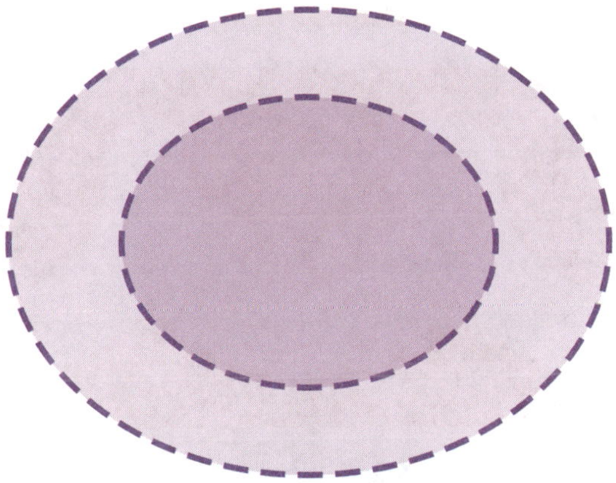

Oval

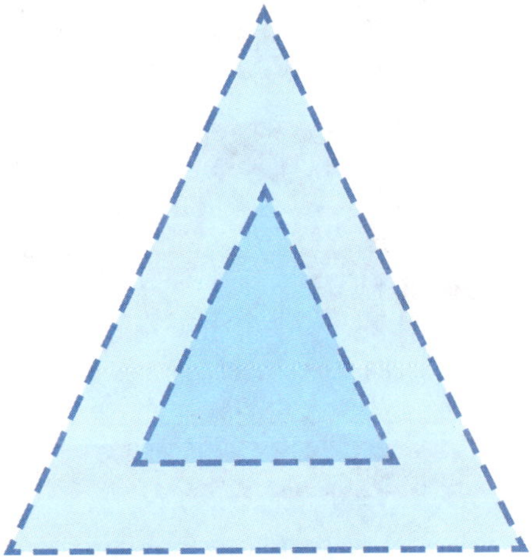

Triangle

Square

Rectangle

LINEUP

Trace the lines from **left** to **right**.

THE LETTER A

A is for **astronaut**.

Practice tracing and writing **A**.

Draw a line from each picture to its beginning sound.

A is for:

A

A

A

THE LETTER B

B is for **boat**.

Practice tracing and writing **B**.

Draw a line from each picture to its beginning sound.

B is for:

B

B

B

THE LETTER C

C is for **carrot**.

Practice tracing and writing **C**.

Draw a line from each picture to its beginning sound.

C is for:

C

C

C

THE LETTER D

D is for **duck**.

Practice tracing and writing **D**.

D D

Draw a line from each picture to its beginning sound.

D is for:

D

D

D

THE LETTER E

E is for **elevator**.

Practice tracing and writing **E**.

E E

Draw a line from each picture to its beginning sound.

E is for:

E

E

E

THE LETTER F

F is for **fish**.

Practice tracing and writing **F**.

1 2 3

Draw a line from each picture to its beginning sound.

F is for:

F

F

F

THE LETTER G

G is for **goldfish**.

Practice tracing and writing **G**.

Draw a line from each picture to its beginning sound.

G is for:

G

G

G

THE LETTER H

H is for **hat**.

Practice tracing and writing **H**.

H H

Draw a line from each picture to its beginning sound.

H is for:

H

H

H

THE LETTER I

I is for **insects**.

Practice tracing and writing **I**.

Draw a line from each picture to its beginning sound.

I is for:

I

I

I

THE LETTER J

J is for **juggler**.

Practice tracing and writing **J**.

Draw a line from each picture to its beginning sound.

J is for:

J

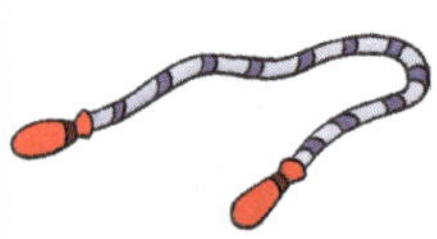

J

J

THE LETTER K

K is for **kangaroo**.

Practice tracing and writing **K**.

Draw a line from each picture to its beginning sound.

K is for:

K

K

K

THE LETTER L

L is for **ladybug**.

Practice tracing and writing **L**.

Draw a line from each picture to its beginning sound.

L is for:

L

L

L

THE LETTER M

M is for **mushrooms**.

Practice tracing and writing **M**.

Draw a line from each picture to its beginning sound.

M is for:

M

M

M

THE LETTER N

N is for **nuts**.

Practice tracing and writing **N**.

Draw a line from each picture to its beginning sound.

N is for:

N

N

N

THE LETTER O

O is for **owl**.

Practice tracing and writing O.

Draw a line from each picture to its beginning sound.

O is for:

O

O

O

THE LETTER P

P is for **pen**.

Practice tracing and writing **P**.

P P

Draw a line from each picture to its beginning sound.

P is for:

P

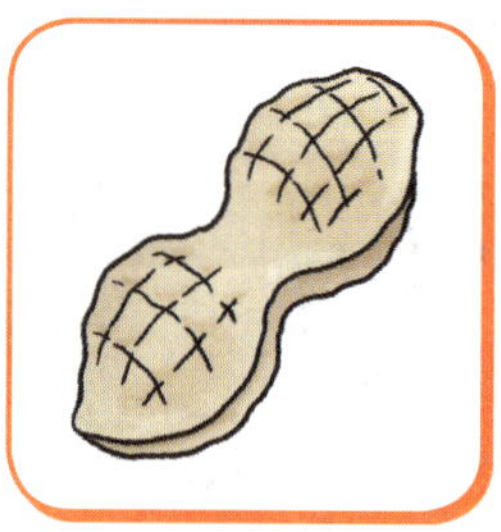

P

P

THE LETTER Q

Q is for **queen**.

Practice tracing and writing **Q**.

Draw a line from each picture to its beginning sound.

Q is for:

Q

Q

Q

THE LETTER R

R is for **rose**.

Practice tracing and writing **R**.

R R

Draw a line from each picture to its beginning sound.

R is for:

R

R

R

THE LETTER S

S is for **seal**.

Practice tracing and writing **S**.

S S

Draw a line from each picture to its beginning sound.

S is for:

S

S

S

THE LETTER T

T is for **teapot**.

Practice tracing and writing **T**.

Draw a line from each picture to its beginning sound.

T is for:

T

T

T

THE LETTER U

U is for **umpire**.

Practice tracing and writing **U**.

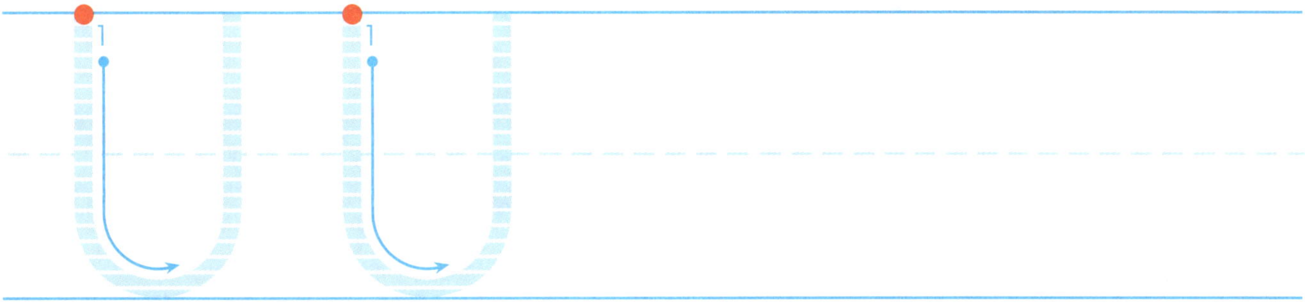

Draw a line from each picture to its beginning sound.

U is for:

THE LETTER V

V is for **vegetables**.

Practice tracing and writing **V**.

Draw a line from each picture to its beginning sound.

V is for:

V

V

V

THE LETTER W

W is for **wagon**.

Practice tracing and writing **W**.

W W

Draw a line from each picture to its beginning sound.

W is for:

W

W

W

THE LETTER X

X is for **x-ray**.

Practice tracing and writing **X**.

Help the pirate ship get to Alligator Island. **X** marks the spot.

THE LETTER Y

Y

is for **yacht**.

Practice tracing and writing **Y**.

Draw a line from each picture to its beginning sound.

Y is for:

Y

Y

Y

THE LETTER Z

Z is for **zipper**.

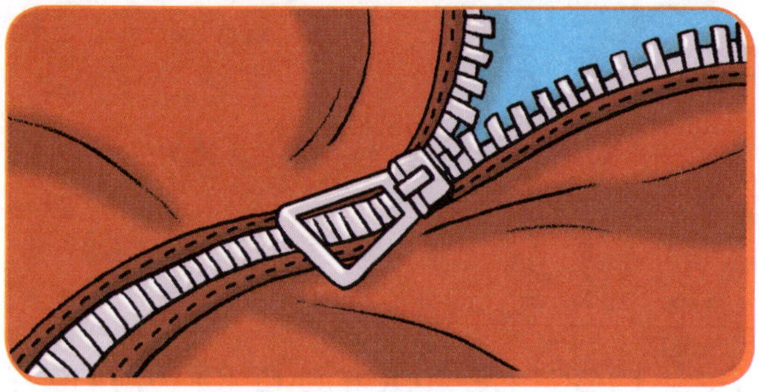

Practice tracing and writing **Z**.

Draw a line from each picture to its beginning sound.

Z is for:

Z

Z

Z

ALPHABET TRACING FUN

Practice tracing the **alphabet**.

HOME SWEET HOME

Help the bird get to its nest.
Draw a line to show the way.

SAME SIZE

These  are the **same size**.

Circle the pictures that are the **same** size.

BIGGER

This  is **bigger** than this .

Circle the picture that is **bigger** than the first one.

SMALLER

This  is **smaller** than this .

Circle the picture that is **smaller** than the first one.

LONG

This  is **longer** than this  .

Circle the bird with the **long** pants.

Circle the bird with the **long** legs.

SHORT

This 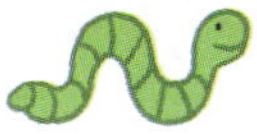 is **shorter** than this 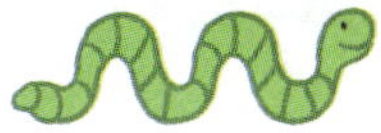 .

Circle the dog with the **short** tail.

Circle the girl with the **short** hair.

WHICH ARE THE SAME?

These are the **same**.

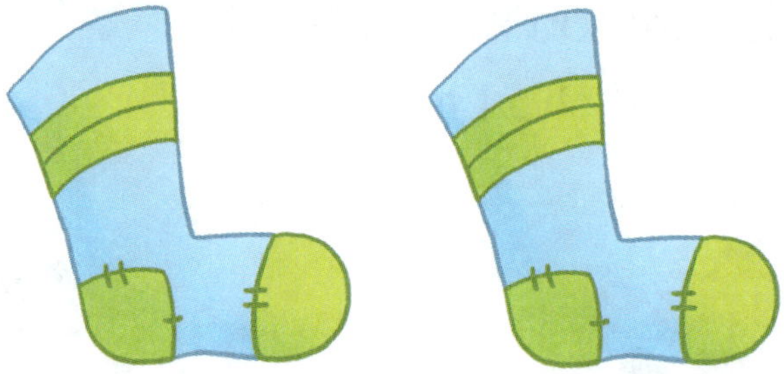

Circle two that are the **same**.

WHICH ARE THE SAME?

Circle two that are the **same**.

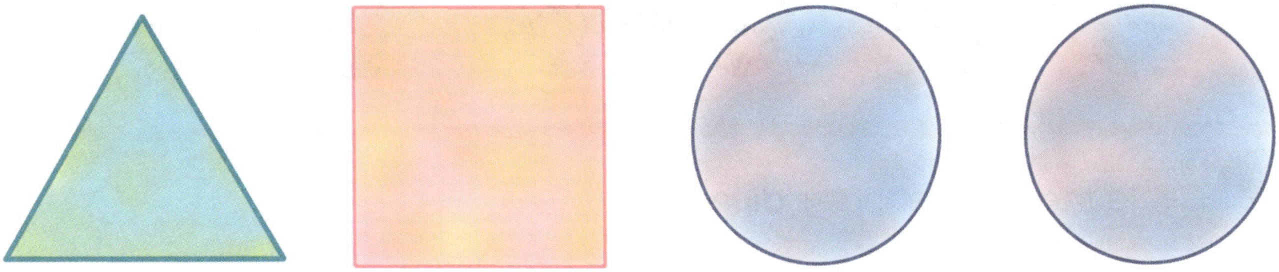

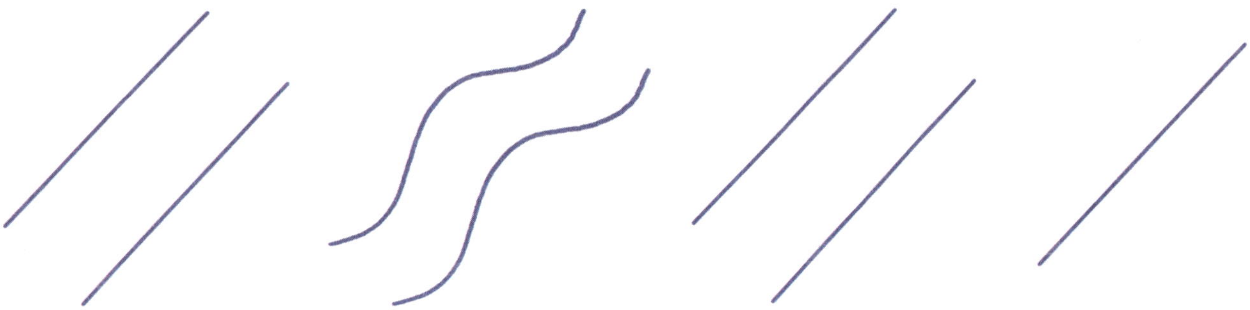

WHICH IS DIFFERENT?

One is **different**.

Circle the picture that is **different**.

WHICH IS DIFFERENT?

Circle the picture that is **different**.

WHAT GOES TOGETHER?

✏ Circle the picture that **belongs** with the first one.

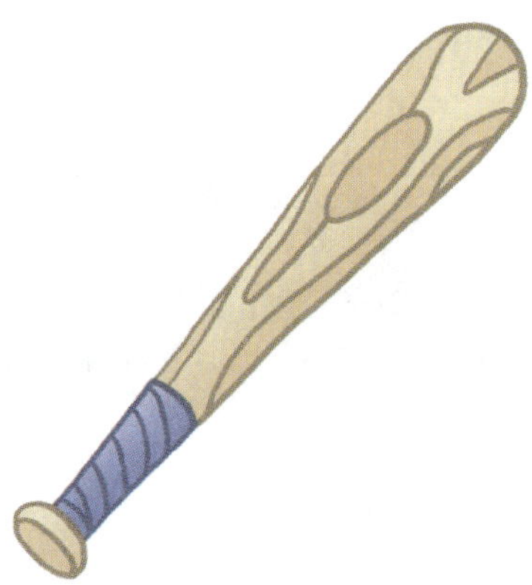

WHAT GOES TOGETHER?

Circle the picture that **belongs** with the first one.

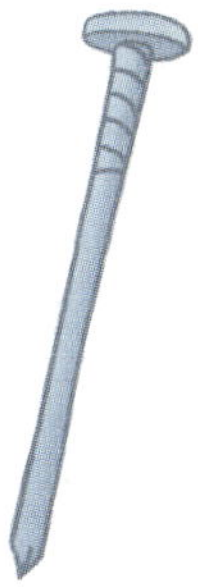
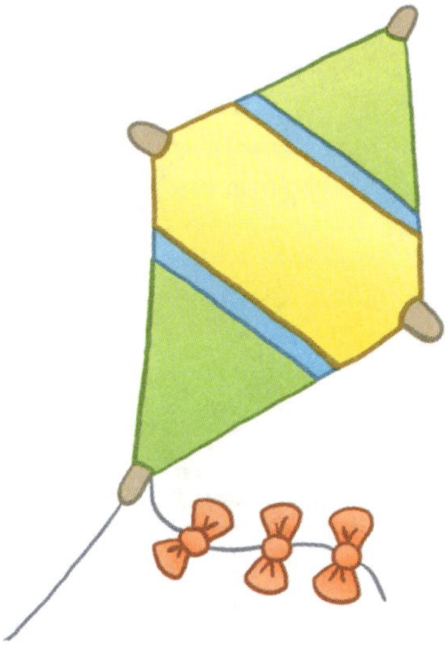

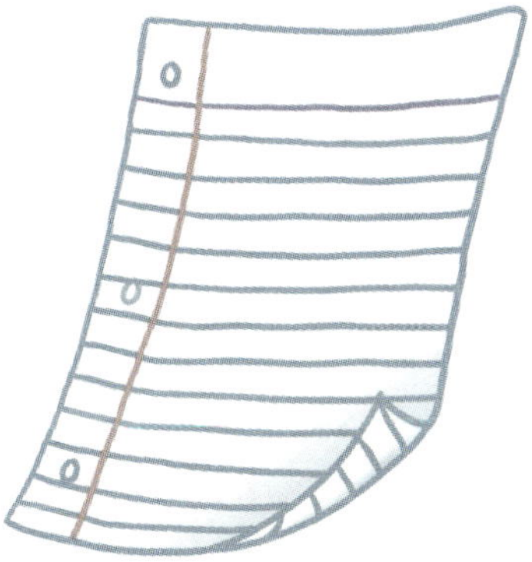
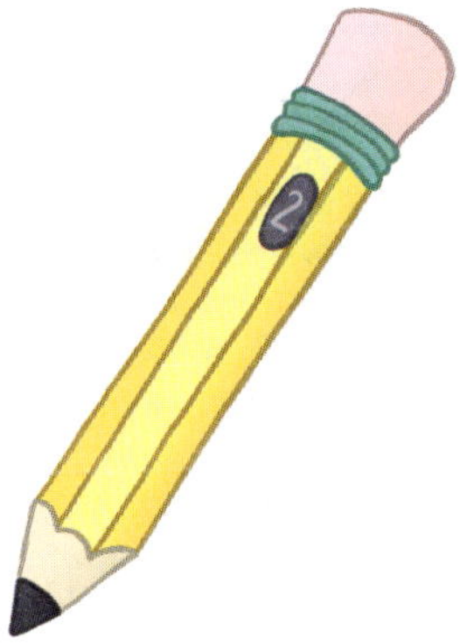

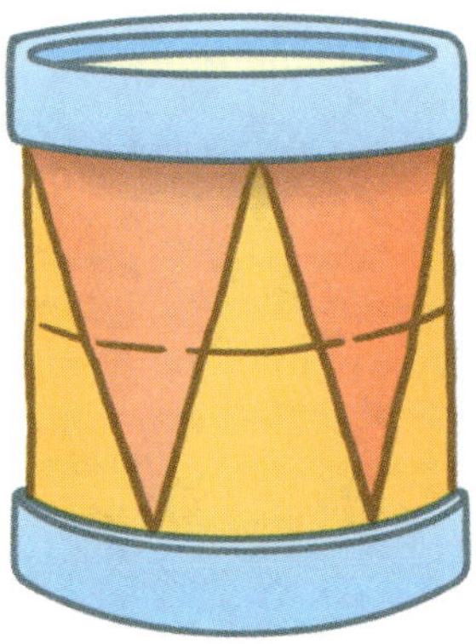

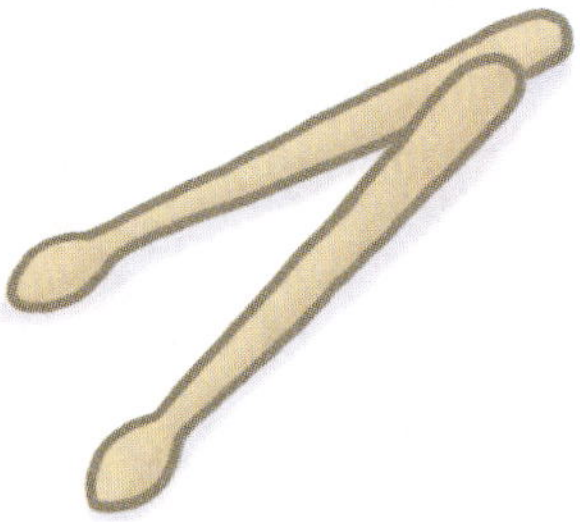

WHAT GOES TOGETHER?

Circle the picture that **belongs** with the first one.

WHAT GOES TOGETHER?

Circle the picture that **belongs** with the first one.

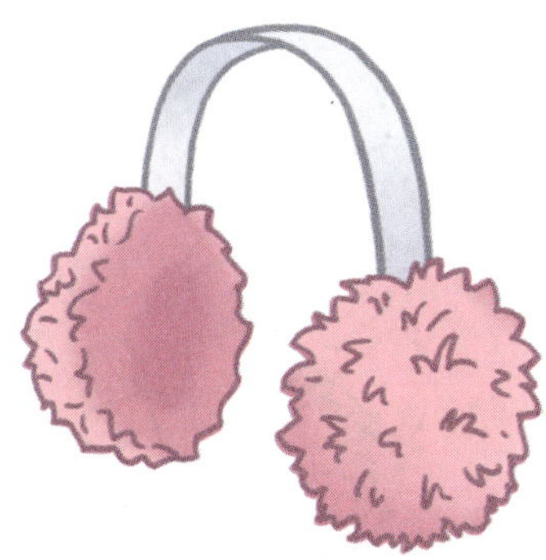

BEAUTIFUL BLUE

Color the  blue.

Color what is blue.

GREAT GREEN

Color the  green.

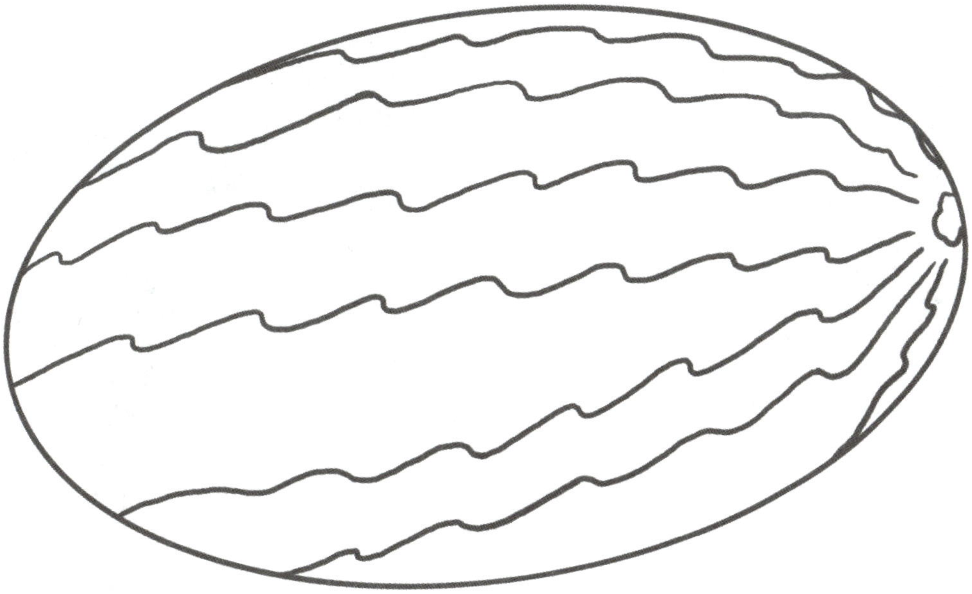

Color what is green.

PERFECT PURPLE

Color the  **purple**.

Color what is **purple**.

REAL RED

Color the  **red**.

Color what is **red**.

OUTSTANDING ORANGE

Color the  **orange**.

Color what is **orange**.

YIPPEE FOR YELLOW!

Color the  yellow.

Color what is yellow.

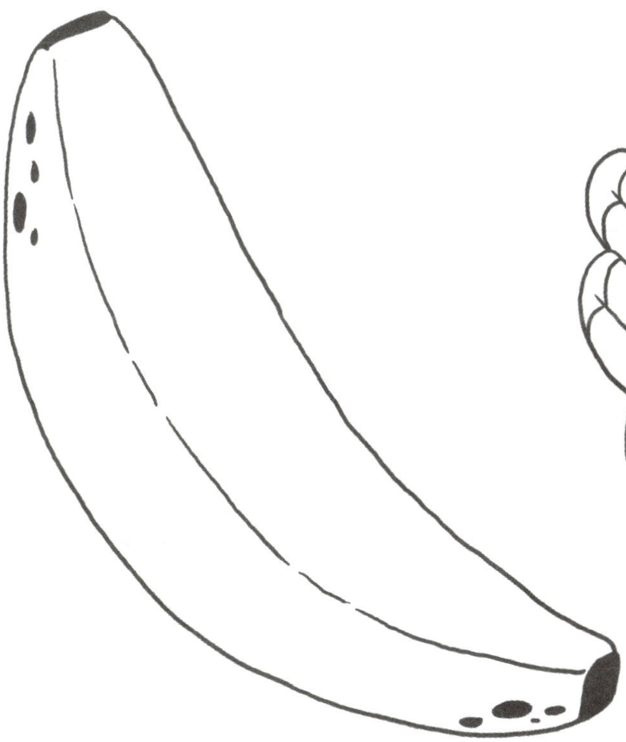

COOL COLORS

Color the  green.

Color the  yellow.

Color the  blue.

Color the  orange.

Color the  red.

Color the  purple.

SUMMER FUN

Circle what you would wear when it is hot outside.

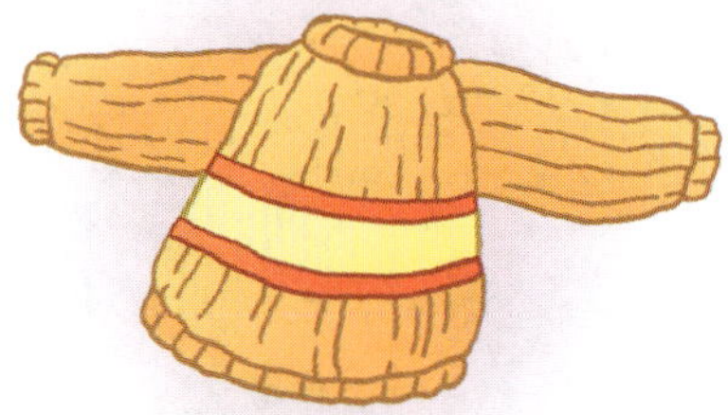

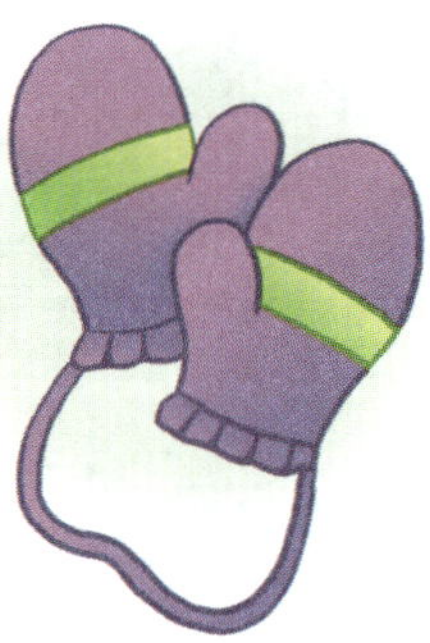

WINTER WEAR

Circle what you would wear when it is cold outside.

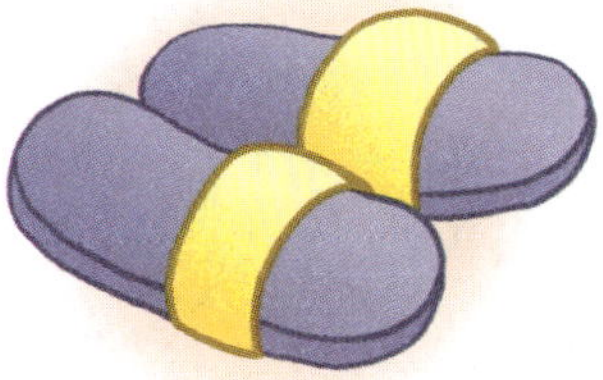

WHERE DOES IT BELONG?

 **belong** in a 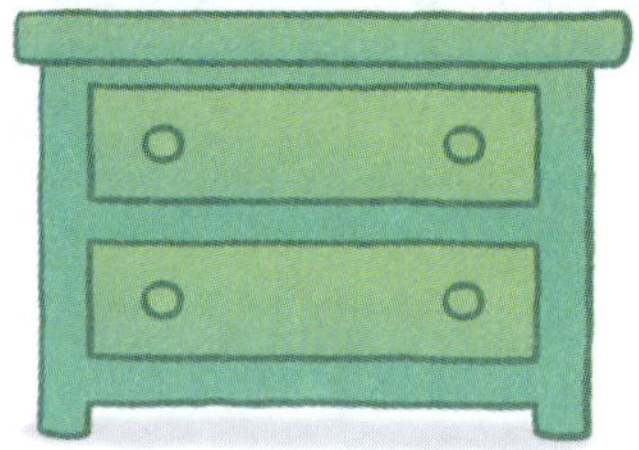

Draw a line to where each thing **belongs**.

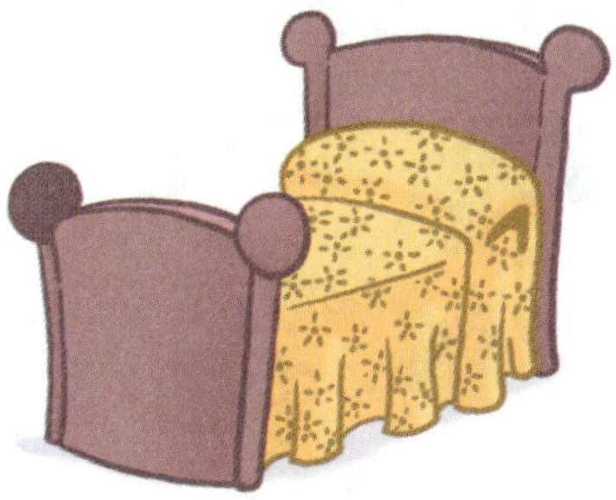

WHERE DOES IT BELONG?

Draw a line to where each thing **belongs**.

WHERE DOES IT BELONG?

Draw a line to where each thing **belongs**.

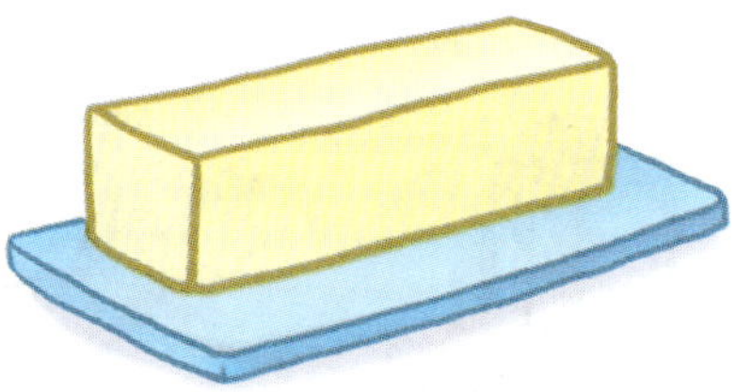

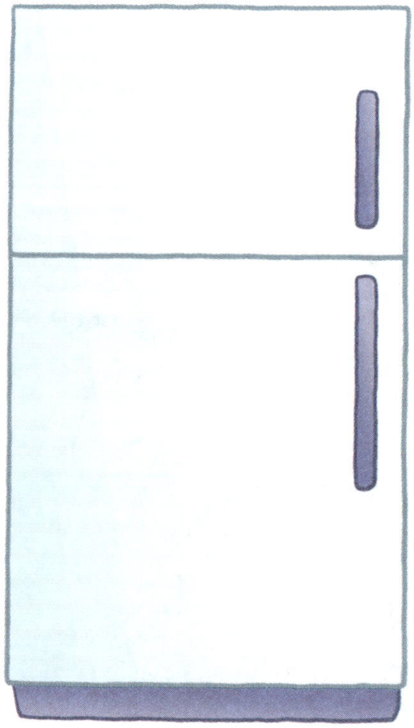

HOW WOULD YOU FEEL?

happy

sad

Circle the face that shows how you would **feel**.

POND PATTERNS

Color the last one to continue the **pattern**.

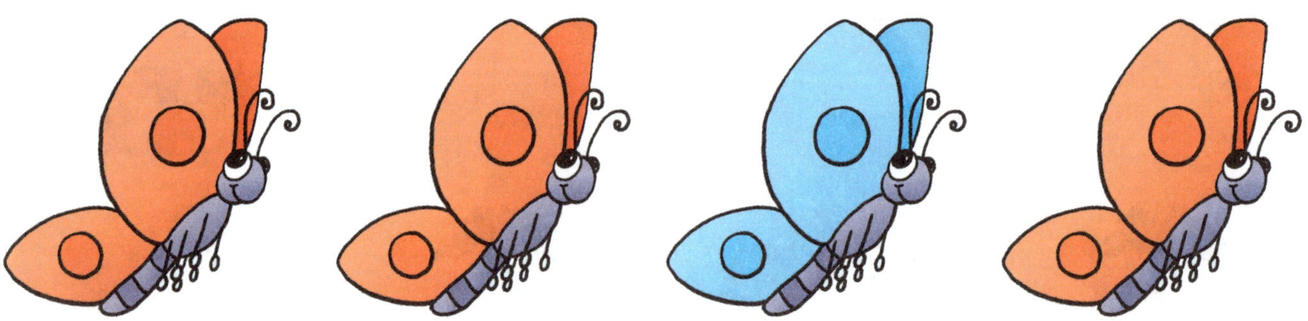

FINDING THE OPPOSITE

In is the **opposite** of **out**.

Circle the picture that shows the **opposite** of the first one.

FINDING THE OPPOSITE

Circle the picture that shows the **opposite** of the first one.

BEGINNING SOUNDS

penguin **p**izza

Circle the picture that begins with the **same sound** as the first one.

monkey

tree

mouse

bird

banana

frog

pig

book

pear

BEGINNING SOUNDS

Circle the picture that begins with the **same sound** as the first one.

turkey

turtle

lemon

ladder

hamburger

lion

nest

firefighter

necklace

BEGINNING SOUNDS

Circle the picture that begins with the **same sound** as the first one.

dog

doll

car

horse

parrot

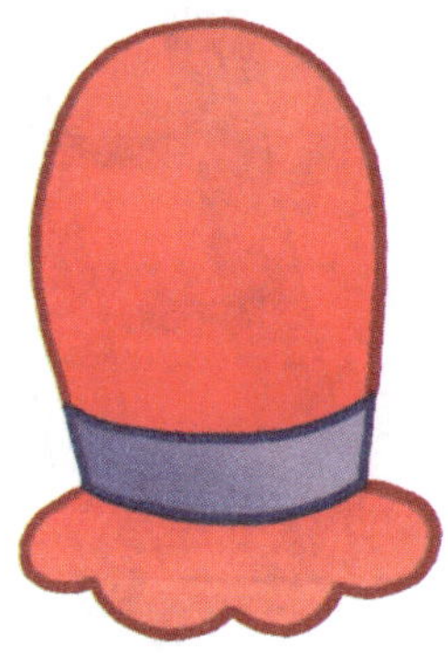

hat

fish

fox

house

BEGINNING SOUNDS

Circle the picture that begins with the **same sound** as the first one.

kangaroo

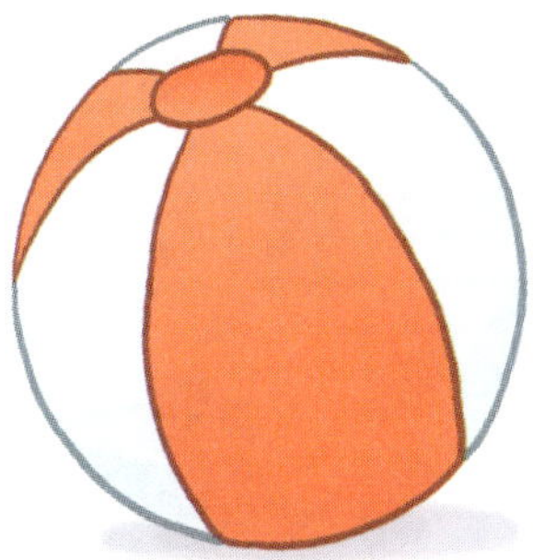

ball

kite

wagon

watch

ring

cat

cow

duck

BEGINNING SOUNDS

Circle the picture that begins with the **same sound** as the first one.

zebra

snake

zipper

alligator

apple

pineapple

octopus

bear

ostrich

BEGINNING SOUNDS

Circle the picture that begins with the **same sound** as the first one.

goat

goose

chicken

rabbit

saw

rake

sun

seal

moon

RHYME TIME

Goat rhymes with **boat**.

Circle the picture that **rhymes** with the first one.

tree

bee

turtle

bear

shoe

pear

cat

duck

hat

MORE RHYME TIME

Circle the picture that **rhymes** with the first one.

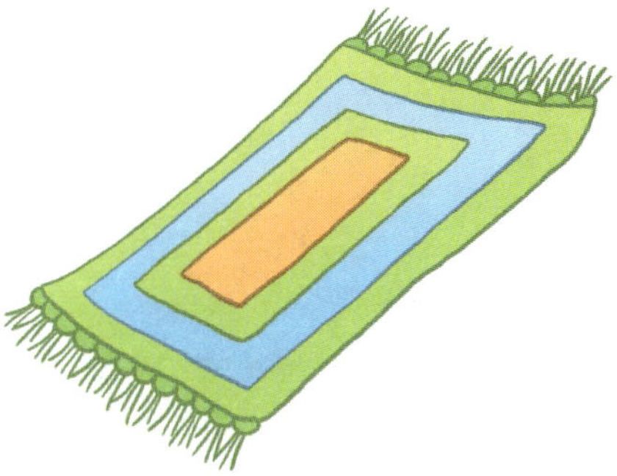

rug

apple

bug

train

car

plane

cake

snake

bird

AT HOME

1

one

Circle the groups of **1**.

ON THE FARM

2
two

Circle the groups of **2**.

ROAD TRIP

3
three

Circle the groups of **3**.

A DAY AT THE BEACH

4
four

Circle the groups of **4**.

TOY STORE

5
five

Circle the groups of **5**.

BIRTHDAY PARTY

6
six

Circle the groups of **6**.

7
seven

Circle the groups of **7**.

8 eight

Circle the groups of **8**.

9

nine

Circle the groups of **9**.

10

ten

Circle the groups of **10**.

How many are on both pages?

Circle the number.

 2 3 4

 2 3 4

 3 4 5

 1 2 3

How many are on both pages?

Circle the number.

apple	6	7	8
flower	7	8	9
butterfly	4	5	6
bee	8	9	10

KEEPING COOL

Connect the dots from **1** to **10**.
Then color the picture.

COUNTING TOYS

Circle the number that shows **how many** there are.

1 2 3

1 2 3

1 2 3

3 4 5

COUNTING FRUIT

Circle the number that shows **how many** there are.

4 5 6

6 7 8

4 5 6

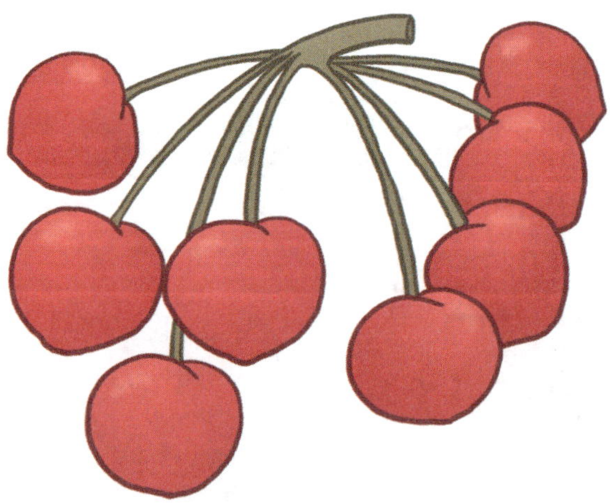

6 7 8

COUNTING CRITTERS

 is the **same** number as 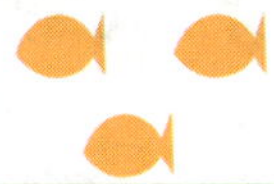.

Circle the group that shows the **same** number as the first one.

ONE MORE

 is **one more** than .

Circle the group that has **one more** than the first one.

ONE FEWER

 is **one fewer** than .

Circle the group that has **one fewer** than the first one.

GREATER THAN

Greater means more than.
5 is **greater** than 4.

Circle the group that is **greater**.

LESS THAN

Less means not as many.
2 is **less** than 3.

Circle the group that has **less**.

FUN FRIEND

Color by numbers to show a picture and a word.

1 = purple 2 = red 3 = orange 4 = green 5 = blue

This is a picture of a ________________________ .

PLAYFUL PAL

Color by numbers to show a picture and a word.

6 = yellow 7 = brown 8 = black 9 = red 10 = blue

This is a picture of a ____________________ .

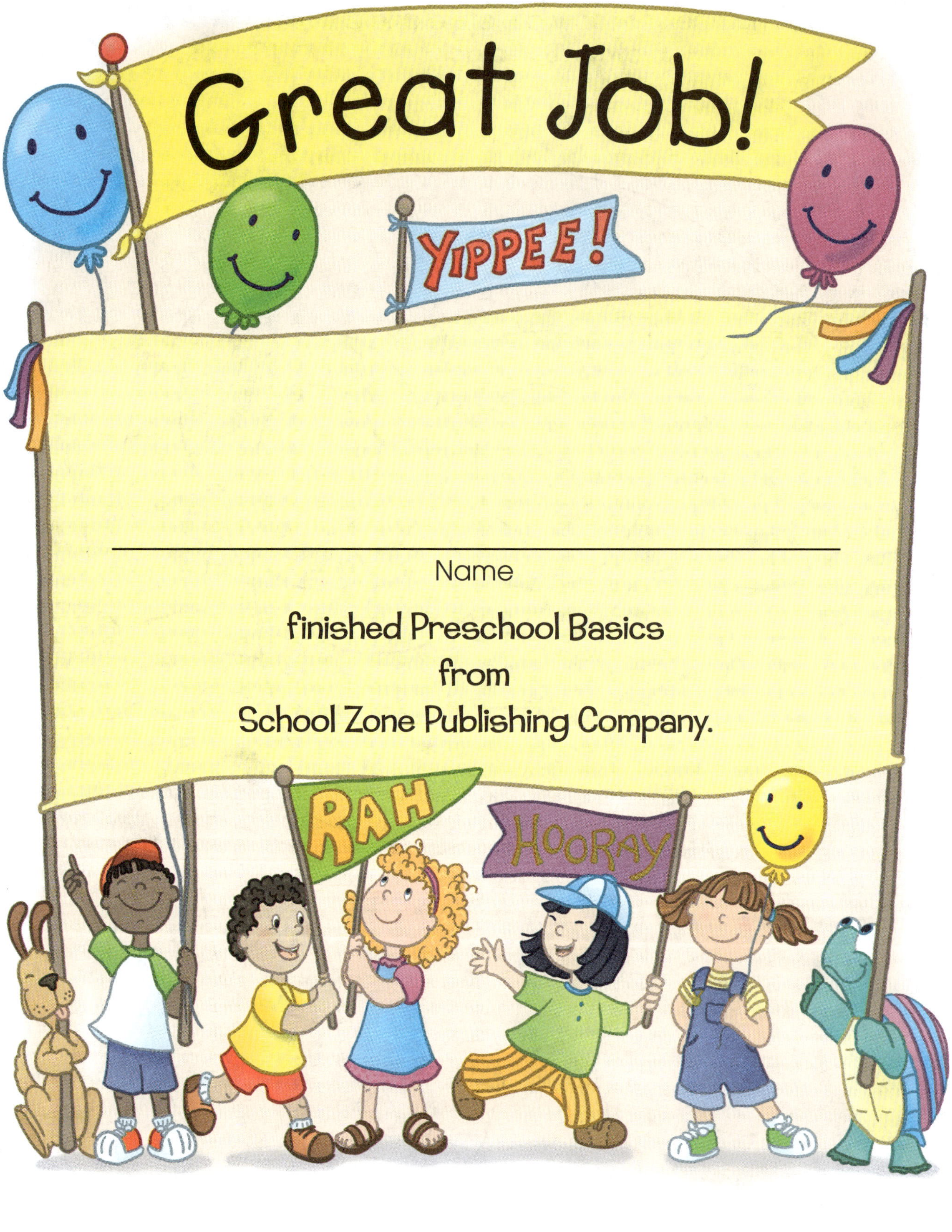
Great Job!
YIPPEE!
Name
finished Preschool Basics
from
School Zone Publishing Company.
RAH
HOORAY